Will Not Come

By

Patrick W Kavanagh

Copyright 2018 Patrick W Kavanagh

INTRODUCTION

Sometimes, we are frozen. We are frozen by grief and frozen by shock. Perhaps, we feel that we are being strong. We are 'holding it together' for ourselves and those we love. We keep a tight grip on our emotions to get us through the loss of a loved one, a broken romance or the unexpected ending of our way of living. We harden our hearts and struggle on, while each day a little piece of us dies.

Tears must come. Without them, we will never release the pain and find healing. Until we let go of the anger, frustration and grief inside of us we will never be fully alive again. Ten years ago, I lost my wife and I fell into deep despair. I withdrew from life and my health began to fail. Each day, I died a little more inside.

Then one day, the first poem appeared from somewhere beyond my conscious mind. I believe that it was guidance from the spirit of my departed wife. Each poem brought tears. Each poem brought healing.

I was encouraged to post my poetry on social media. The many comments which I have received over the past six years have convinced me that the messages which I have passed on have provided a source of comfort and healing to those who are suffering from depression and grief. Many also relate to coping with our own illness and that of loved ones. They seem to contain a wisdom which is beyond my conscious awareness and I believe that they can provide a valuable resource for those who wish to live a more inspired and fulfilling life.

Patrick W Kavanagh
November 2018

AKNOWLEDGEMENTS

Many thanks to all the lovely people who have supported my work. Thank you all for the heart-warming comments.

Victoria F, "Thank you! so needed right now."

Christine Y, "Beautiful and powerful"

Barbara D, "Meaningful, wonderful and very true. Thank you for this."

Shirley M, "I needed to read this today. Thank you."

Karen T F, "Love this……Thank You."

June W, "Thank you and so true for me"

Katie E, "If sorrow could be beautiful, it would sound like this."

Jane C, "Your words make my heart sing, thank you."

Allen D B, "Inspirational and reflective, thank you for sharing."

Ali R, "Thank you for those beautiful words, Patrick"

Elizabeth H. J, "This is beyond awesome, Patrick."

Adrienne T, "Thank you for this beautiful poem… a wonderful start to my day."

Shonda B. "Very touching, inspirational!"

Clive F, "So inspirational"

Marie S, "Wonderful, thank you."

Kim H, "Wonderful!"

Mary L, "Powerful. Well said."

Eva E. B, "Am I allowed to read out to a group at church? It is so beautiful. Thank you."

Sara M-H, "Wow speechless!"

Sharon H, "MAGNIFICENT!!!"

Jane W, "Very chilling, and seems so real."

Carol T, "Wow, that's chilling and awesome!"

Jenni B, "Wonderful, gave me goose bumps!"

Jane C, "Once again you have brought beauty to my morning. Thank you"

Prentiss M, "Marvellous, absolute truth. Love you brother, BB."

Amanda M. R, "Very beautiful, touching words. Thank you"

Kelsey S, "Love your hope, sadness, acceptance."

Annabel B, "Beautiful once again…"

April W, "Blessings, simply beautiful. Thank you, I needed this today."

Leta D, "Wise words my dear brother. I know them for the truth. As youth and vigour are left behind for experience and knowledge. A wistfulness falls upon me as I ponder today's youth.

Vlatka P, "Such beautiful words of wisdom my friend… thank you so much…"

David M, "Beautiful"

Donna H, "Thank you. This is such a beautiful testimony to real love."

Maponos M, "This is really beautiful. There is so much truth and insight here...Well done... thanks for sharing it..."

Debi R, "Perfect, Patrick! Your words are always so evocative."

Laura MacD, "This is beautiful, powerful and emotive. May I share this? There are some people I know who need these words."

Eugene B, "Quite enthralling. Deeply moving."

Sharon B, "Wonderful words and feelings, made me cry, beautiful"

Sandra J. B, "Love it, you are the best, I have not come across one of your pieces that I have not liked. Thank-you for sharing the beautiful writing you do, I feel very privileged to be reading such wonderful work."

Candice W, "Thinking of one who has loved and lost...this is perfect."

Donna H, "I do walk with you Patrick. Your wonderful words take me with you as we take this journey called "life". Thank you for sharing them here so that I and others can "walk with you" a way."

Ian M, "Powerful words Patrick. Yet again your lines sum up the subject matter better than a hundred-page essay."

I would love to list everyone, and all the lovely comments which have uplifted me, but space does not allow it. Thank you everybody on social media for all your love and support over the past ten years.

Patrick W Kavanagh
December 2018

BE GENTLE

Be gentle with your heart,
The world can change within a single beat.
Tread lightly in the world,
And treat with kindness, all the people you may meet.

Wisdom costs us dearly,
The price that we must pay, - we pay in sorrow and in loss.
And all the times we try, - we ask ourselves the reason why,
But still, we carry on the burden of survival, for the sake of those we love.
And gaze in silent question at the grey and sullen sky.

Rage against the storms that carry all we love away.
Turn your back against the setting sun that leaves us cold, or hungry or alone at end of day.
Shake your fist and cry out to the moon, - howling out with sorrow like the solitary wolf.
Touch the earth with dewy tears as sunrise makes us face another day.
But still the earth will turn, and we will heal, - for that is nature's way.

Patrick W Kavanagh
27/12/2013

WHEN I AM ALONE

When my sadness tells me that there's nothing left inside.
When life has lost its joy and all I want to do is run and hide.
When bitterness and sorrow poison everything I do.
The one remaining comfort in my lonely life is you.

I walk the quiet streets and I can feel you everywhere.
I feel your gentle presence in the cool night breeze that lays a kiss upon my hair
I hear you in the rustle of the Autumn leaves that swirl around me as I walk.
You listen to my every word when, finally, I find the will to talk.

Who but you can lead me safely home when I am lost?
Who is always there to rescue me and never counts the cost?
You are the one who answers every question if I only listen to the things you have to say.
You are there when sleep has fled and all I have is dread-filled thoughts about the coming days.

When you have raised my spirits high you share in all my joys.
You are the warmth of Summer's sun, - the shimmering blue in Summers sunny skies.
You are the Way, the Truth and all of Life. You are the love that sparkles in a stranger's eyes.
You are the tongue which always speaks the truth, - the tongue that never lies.

There is nothing I must do to please you, - but to feel you I must resonate your love.
It is written in the stars that everything I do below reflects in all the worlds above.
Your wisdom, deep inside me, tells me that I must become the world I wish to see.
Your patience tells me, that if I should fail a thousand times,
Your love still waits for me.

Patrick W Kavanagh

27/09/2017

A REST FROM THE ROAD

 A long hot summer day was cooling when I reached the little inn.
Light enough to travel on a little further, but the likes of this unlikely resting place, I might not find again.
I leave my pack inside the little door and wander to the bar,
A strange excitement overtakes me as I ask about a room, and talk about my travels to the barman, - who asks me if my journey took me far.

 The old man soaked up all the sunlight from the tiny window as he gazed with sadness at his empty glass and muttered something soft and low.
I offered him a pint of stout by way of rent and went to share the warmth beneath the shining beams of golden evenings glow.
I had scarce sat down before my tithe had disappeared, and so I called for one more round.
Then as the Guinness reached its mark, a smile began to grow on those parched lips that hitherto had frowned.

 "My name is Jack," he said, - so suddenly I jumped and banged my head on blacked beams that drooped and yawed without a care.
This tiny inn had little sympathy for careless travellers who stood too tall and brushed the cobwebbed ceiling with their hair.
The cautious smile became a hearty laugh, and years of hardship seemed to vanish from his face.
And as I rubbed my aching head, he told me how he came to be in such a place.

 "I walked the highways and the byways of this land since I was just a hairless youth.
I never needed more than just one pair of brogues, a well-waxed cape and just one woollen suit.
I played the fiddle for my keep, and many lasses placed an ardent kiss upon my lips behind the old inn door.
And happy was the life I led until I fell in love with Rosie Moore".

"Her father was a wealthy farmer in these parts who cared not much for travellers like me.
But Rosie was an impish rogue who longed to love and yearned to travel far and free.
We ran away one moonlit night, and met beside the crossroads, underneath the gallows tree.
Sure, maybe it was choosing such a place that well might make an end of me".

Her father and his men were waiting for us there, and I was caught before I had a chance.
Poor Rosie had a beating as he dragged her home without a second glance.
Then the rope appeared and in that awful moment, I discovered what it meant to fear.
They made a simple noose around my neck and pulled it taut and left me swinging there.

I thought my life was over. I could hear them laughing as they left me there to die.
But as their voices ebbed into the night a shifting shadow caught my eye.
My Rosie had escaped, and when she cut me down, she washed my wounds with salty tears,
We wandered far and wide as man and wife for many happy years.

We walked the highways and the byways, 'till I saved enough to buy a horse and caravan.
We were never blessed with children, but for all of that, she never made me feel that I was lacking as a man.
I played my fiddle for our keep at every wedding, funeral and feast.
It was just enough to feed us both and shoe our faithful beast.

We were famous, in our way, and stopped at many farms without suspicion, scorn or fear.
Our days were filled with laughter and untouched by any tears.
I felt I was the richest man alive, - for who could ask for more than lovely Rosie by his side?
It seemed my joy might last forever, - 'til my lovely Rosie died.

We halted at the woodlands near the bridge, the Winter before last.
Poor Rosie caught a fever and by spring, her time had passed.
The parish laid her to her rest on hallowed ground, and even put my words upon a stone.
I promised her that where she lay would be my final home.

I sold my beast, and all the village came to help me say goodbye.
Her spirit would still have a home. The embers of our caravan reached high into the sky.
It's waiting there for me when sorrow lets me leave to be there by her side.
And, we will travel Heaven's roads just like we did when she was first my bride.

I saw the teardrops glaze his eyes and left him to his sorrow as I went back to the bar.
He brightened up a little as he saw the pints of Guinness and I handed him a 'jar'.
He downed his pint and wished me health, then drifted off into eternal sleep.
And as his breathing slowed and stopped, I raised my glass to say goodbye,
And tried hard not to weep.

Patrick W Kavanagh
13/08/2014

MY TEARS MAY NEVER END

My tears may never end.
At least they fill the numbness which I used to call a heart
My tears may never end.
And I cannot envision how to make another start.
Your sympathy just brings me further pain.
Because the treasure I have lost can never come again

My tears may never end.
I understand that you are simply trying to be a helpful friend.
My tears will never end.
And you will never understand the hell to which we must descend.
I try hard to be strong for everyone who's left behind.
But I have lost the will to carry on and almost lost my mind.

How can I feel love again/?
The love I bore has brought more pain than anyone can bear.
How can I feel love again?
I look to where you lay each night and you're no longer there.
The loss of faith in losing you is greater than the worst despair.
My heart is torn beyond belief, - is torn beyond repair.

I want to hope, I want to dream.
I want so badly to believe this loss is not as final as it seems.
I want my night to turn back into day.
I want to find the path ahead, but I can't see the way.
I want to cherish all that's left behind,
But rage and overwhelming sorrow blacken every day.

Should I bow to sadness?
Let it sweep the darkness and the bitterness away?
Should I bow to sorrow?
Let my tears wash all my accusations and my angry thoughts away?
Should I bow to God?
Or curse him for the tragedy that swept my love away?
Should I bow to Fate?
Should I try to tell myself there was no other way?

I am not ready to heal.
I am not prepared to let these hellish moments pass and simply fade away.
I am not ready yet to say goodbye and simply walk away.
You were my heart and all my life, and I will not be healed so soon.
I will clutch your memories and all that I have left until my dying day.
Then, when once again I see your smiling face,
I will know that every moment born of love can never fade away.

Patrick W Kavanagh
20/05/2018

SOMEONE IN THE WORLD WAS FEELING SAD

Someone in the world was feeling very sad. I wondered, "was it you?"
Someone near, - or very far, was feeling just the way you are. I wondered what to do.
Someone had those lonely thoughts which slip right in between the busy thoughts we use to block them out.
Someone in this lovely, lonely word was feeling sad, - as those who love so deeply, often do.

You are a warrior, - no matter how you feel right now, - no matter what you say!
You are a winner even though you feel that you have lost, some days.
You are a child of stardust underneath the doubt and fear and pain.
You are immortal and once more you'll spin the dice and come again.

Are we so wise, - that we should know these truths about the world?
I think that deep inside we are a calm still pool where Spirits energy can swirl.
Below the worries and above the stresses and distractions of our busy restless days,
There stands a bright and beneficent being who lights, for us, the way.

Do not fear, for everything will pass in its good time and sorrow is a fleeting thing.
Before the universe has breathed it's last, - you may be a pauper or a poet or a king.
Joy and happiness will come and, surely, sorrow once again will have its share.
It only matters that we live our lives with love and live a life of kindness and of care.

Patrick W Kavanagh
05/05/2018

DANCE IN THE SUN

"You are dying too soon," the old man said.
I looked down in despair at his wrinkled, old head.
"I am young! I am strong, yet we neither have long."
He laughed! Then he croaked out his tattered old song.

"I am free! I am free! Like the birds and the bees.
I've not long left to walk on these crippled old knees.
My trials and my troubles are soon to be done!
I will wear a new body and dance in the sun."

You're a fool!" I replied as I knelt by his side.
"There is nothing but bones in your wrinkled old hide.
The body you wish for, - it never will be.
I will not be fooled by the vision you see."

Each bone of his fingers was etched on my palm.
He said, "I am leaving, and you must be calm.
Reside in the silence and peace of the day.
My freedom is here, and I must be away."

His smile was the gift which he left as he passed.
I knelt, and I pondered his decades long past.
That my own death was coming, - I already knew.
The doctors had told me there's nothing to do.

How could he smile as his life bled away?
I pondered this question for all of that day.
No answer forthcoming, - but yet, I could see.
His passing was calmer than any I'd seen.

That year went so quickly, - it passed in a blur.
My portended death simply did not occur.
I felt he had gifted the last of his power,
To help a young man in his darkest of hours.

Now all my grown children are sat 'round my bed.
They gaze down in sadness at my wrinkled head.
I tell them, " My life was a gift from beyond.,
And now I must leave you to dance in the sun."

Patrick W Kavanagh
20/11/2016

THERE IS A WORLD

There is a world where leafy lanes are garlanded with purple flowers.
There is a world where tall trees reach up to a sky of baby blue.
Where cotton clouds drift slowly over morning fields of green, green grass,
Which sparkle with a million hazy spider's webs, that catch the morning dew.

There is a world where crystal springs flow cool and pure and clear.
They splash against the mossy rocks and ripple in among the reeds that gently wave.
A world where snowy mountains scrape the heavens, stretching high above the clouds.
Where sandy beaches stretch for miles, and the salty air is booming with the sound of crashing waves.

There is a world where every living creature lives in balance with the wonders all around.
A world where all mankind is equal, and where all mankind is free.
A world where death is just a door, a thoroughfare to something more.
A world that waits to reappear, when you and I agree.

Listen to the piper as he plays for you beneath a sparkling moon.
You will leave behind the things you thought you knew, - enchanted by his tune.
Travel with him, far away, and find a bright new world when you return at dawn of day.
When you have changed the world within, - the change you seek will not be far away.

Patrick W Kavanagh
28/01/2014

THE DARKEST NIGHT

In your darkest night, hold fast to all your memories of laughter, love and light.
Clutch the faded rose and smell the faint perfume of happiness long past.
Feel, once more, the sunlight on your face the day you laughed and danced with pure delight.
That blessed day when love first called your name, and you believed that happiness would last.

Cherished memories inside an antique cabinet of smoky glass and polished wood.
You sit there, gazing through a crystal goblet at a single candle, on a table set for one.
You know the one for whom you long, would be here with you, - if they only could.
But who could tell, that joy so quickly won, would die before the wedding day was done.

You see him still across the years, - a handsome man with hair of straw and courage in his eyes.
He fought in that great war, - the war to end all wars, - it took his life away.
The truck was waiting even as you shared your vows, - then kissed and said goodbye.
Virtues chains left only tears as memories of that sad wedding day.

Fifty years of loss and quiet desperation as the hands of time spun slowly by.
Finally, the time has come to let the sadness gently drift away.
Slipping silently into that other world with no more tears to cry
You gaze around the mausoleum, that you once called your home, and say goodbye.

The candle fades into a gentle light that draws you to its flame.
Like a moth, you fly into its glowing heart and touch your youth again.
There before you, stands your one true love, the cause of all your joy and pain.
And as you fall into each other's arms, another life begins.

Patrick W Kavanagh
11/12 2014

FADED PHOTOGRAPHS

All we loved and lost in this brief world is never far away, though we may be blinded by our tears.
Looking at the faded photographs that span and sweep across so many, many years.
Snippets of our past in pictures spread ...across the world-wide-web, bring many happy tears.
Boxes full of frozen lives, in sepia and black and white, that hint of long-lost years.

They have not left us, - all those moments lying still upon our photographs and our screens.
Time is an illusion, and every moment still exists beyond the Ego's poor, dim sight.
Those we loved, - the ones who travelled on beyond the veil, are standing there unseen.
Sending love and guidance as we struggle through the restless, sleepless nights.

Some of us are locked in memories, but there is joy, still to be found, in this dark world.
Childhood tales still warm our hearts, and every day a whole new world is born.
As we drift into a reverie, we find the doors to inner worlds that set our spirit free.
We find that place where past and future meet, and greet a bright new dawn.

Let us raise our glasses to the brave and strong, who passed away in days now gone.
They lived and died to build a better world, and all their hopes are carried in our bones.
We never won that final war to end all wars and put the world to rights.
But we are fighting still, - and in the end, we'll find our way back home.

Patrick W Kavanagh
13/12/2014

YOU AND ME

I remember you and me when we were skimming stones and climbing gnarly trees.
I remember Summers days of Summer rains and faces swept by Summers fragrant breeze.
Cycle rides beneath those bright blue skies which quickly turned to rain.
Journeys here and journeys there and journeys back again.

I remember you and me when we were bored and restless teens.
Motorbikes and drink and fights and flared out denim jeans.
Racing hard and fast along the mountain tracks in noisy, flash, machines.
Life was made of laughter, lust and ever-changing dreams.

I remember when we dreamt that life would last forever and of our all our dreams unfolding one by one.
But those crazy Summers passed so quickly that they seemed to disappear before they hardly had begun.
Still, there were many other friends who came to decorate my life each time I had to make a brand-new start.
Some who swiftly came and some who swiftly left and some who'll live forever in my heart.

Patrick W Kavanagh
19/12/2017

THE SHINING PATH

Sit beside me, love, and let me hear you sing once more.
The road ahead is calling, I can see the open door.
When I close my eyes, I see it stretching out into the endless night.
A silver path between the trees that glows with mystic light.

Trying not to breathe too deep, I catch the scent of orchids in the calm night air.
And, though I feel your hand in mine, in many ways I am already there.
Underneath the smiling moon, whose halo spreads across the shimmering sky.
The twinkling stars illuminate the wispy clouds that slowly wander by.

What a peaceful night to pass into the glory, that beyond the heavens lies.
Although I hate to leave, there is a light of wonder in my dimming eyes.
As I slowly drift beyond the reach of all the joys and all the sorrows of the day.
I feel your final kiss upon my lips and gently slip away.

Do not cry for me, my love. A perfect passing crowned my life with bliss.
I will always have my time with you and I will always tremble at that final kiss.
Should it pass that I must face, once more, this world of beauty, fear and pain.
I know the fates will draw us to each other, and, one day,
 I'll I hold you to my breast again.

Patrick W Kavanagh
26/03/2014

SPEAK TO ME OF LOVE

Speak to me of love and let me see your light shine gently from above.
The darkness and the solitude have overcome my fleeting sense of hope.
Yesterday, I was so sure that death was just an open door which led to pathways, - barely known.
Today, my certainty has flown away. My life is filled with sadness and I feel so tired and so alone.

Come to me once more and lift my spirits with your perfect smile.
Sometimes, when I walk the streets at night, I hear your laughter in the cool, clear air.
I hear your footsteps close behind me and I slip into the past for just a while,
But, when I turn around in thoughtless joy, - I never find you there.

Come to me and tell me of the Summer lands where all is peace and joy.
I miss the music of your voice so much that silence is the only sound that I can bear.
Speak to me of wondrous things and let me see your angel wings spread out to touch the sky.
Help me comprehend this cruel twist of faith, - I've tried so hard but I can't understand the reason why.

I am not angry. There is nothing to be gained from chiding you for leaving me behind.
But you adorned my life and gave this empty heart a reason to go on.
I sometimes wonder who is with you, on the other side of that invisible divide.
I wonder if you're growing up or growing wiser and what mysteries, you'll find.

I am sorry if my bitterness and grief have blinded me to your immortal light.
I know you never want to see me cry, but sometimes tears are all the comfort that I have.
This world has neither time enough to heal nor sleep enough to get me through the night.
But I believe that I will hold your hand again one day in that new world where only Love holds sway.

Patrick W Kavanagh
20/11/2017

IT IS ALWAYS TOO SOON

It is always too soon.
When you abandon us to sorrow in this world of passing dreams.
All we feel is grief although we sometimes think that nothing is exactly as it seems.
You stand in front of us with arms spread wide to offer an embrace,
But we are blind and cannot even see your loving face.

You are born again into a new reality and you have left this fleeting world behind, -
But we are blind and deaf and dumb, - there is no fault to which we won't succumb.
You travel to a thousand worlds and try to share with us the wisdom that you find.
And though you call us softly in our dreams, -
The morning comes, and we cannot remember what you said or what it means.

"The caterpillar lives in terror of his wings and all the changes that a new life brings.
The chrysalis awakens to a world of mystery and flight.
When your bright new dawn arises in its glory, - when your liberated spirit sings,
Then the only sorrow you will feel is for your loved ones who still struggle in the night.
There is no place for sadness in the world where spirit soars and angels sing"

"In our joyful world, - each heart is bare, and all can see the love that's beating there.
In this place beyond the reach of greed, - there is no loneliness and no despair.
There are lessons to be learned and choices still, - that we must make.
But every heart is free from fear and all the pain which follows in its wake.
Your heart is yearning now, but you will grieve no more, - when you awake."

ANGELS IN THE WIND

I stand and feel the wind's embrace, - as kisses, soft as feathers, touch my smiling face.
Gentle laughter, hushed as falling snow is calling, - and it leads me where I need to go.
Swirling leaves are blowing all around, -that somehow leave a gleaming trace.
But as the seasons meet within my heart, I feel a joy, an all-consuming grace.

It grieves me little now to say that all I think I know will, someday, pass away.
It does not matter that the world will turn, and all my dreams may die and never be reborn.
This perfect moment is enough, within the pause between the night time and the day.
With tiny angels dancing all around in laughter and in play.

"Walk with us between the worlds and let imagination fly.
We will show that all who ever lived, will never die.
We will heal your aching heart and help you understand,
That only love can heal the world and soothe the heart of man."

Patrick W Kavanagh
16/11/2015

JUST FOR TODAY

Just for today, I am resolved to listen to the trees.
Even here within this room, I hear them whisper in the breeze.
They speak of Summer's now long past.
They tell me that the song of life will last.
But now the time has come to settle into Winter's gentle peace.

Even now, the leaves are swirling 'round the windowpane.
They called to say goodbye and promise that they will be back again.
I softly sigh a sweet goodbye
To all of Summer's passing Joys.
And gaze out at the leaden skies which soon will bring the rain.

Suddenly, my eyes are dazzled as the Autumn sun bursts through the clouded sky.
I feel as if Persephone, herself, has called to say goodbye.
Osiris lights the world with sparkling reds and golds.
As if to set a fitting tableau for his lover to behold.
And Hades waits with bated breath to witness, once again, his rivals death.

Just for today, I am determined to accept each moment as it flows.
Just like the past, the future is a dream, and where we will awaken,- no one knows.
The wheel of life will turn and, soon enough, the Beltane fires will burn.
And I will keep the warmth of Summer in my heart until my love returns.
With all the beauty and the joy for which the Winter yearns.

Patrick W Kavanagh
31/10/2016

SO MANY DREAMS

So many dreams I dreamed of all the things we would do.
So many dreams I dreamed and many of those dreams were dreams of you.
So many dreams I dreamed that I would build a world much better than the world I knew.
So many dreams I dreamed for us that never did come true.

I dreamed about a bright new world which I was much too young to understand.
I dreamed so much but there was so much I had yet to learn before I'd be a man.
I dreamed about a life that would be filled with laughter and with love and joy
I dreamed that I could take the world by storm for us, - but I was still a boy.

Dreams are never lies, - not even if they don't come true.
Dreams are never wasted, - for sometimes, to dream is all that we can do.
Dreams can raise us up above the cold hard light of day.
Dreams, sometimes, can be the only beacons left to light our way.

Perhaps my dreams will fade away and vanish like the mist when I am gone.
Perhaps my dreams will find a world more fitting if, somehow, I am reborn.
Perhaps my dreams were never meant to be and simply kept my wounded heart alive.
Perhaps the dreams I share may help my wounded brothers and my wounded sisters to survive.

Patrick W Kavanagh
12/10/2017

THE DAY OF THE DEAD

I stand beneath the moonlit trees to watch and wait for you.
Despite the stealth of his approach, I know that Wolf is waiting too.
You, who were my future and my dreams, have now become my past.
I cry out daily to my Father in the sky to help this sorrow pass.

I, who had the strength of ten, am feeble now with grief.
I stumble through the day when once my step would never stir the leaves.
You, who were my treasure and my joy, have now become my curse.
I was once a warrior, but now each day my weakness and my pain grow slowly worse.

In the coming days and nights, our worlds draw close and you can visit us once more.
If the gods are kind, then I may see you laugh and dance with glee as once you did before.
Although our lodges are all gone, I placed your favourite toys inside our wooden shack,
I also left some sweets and tasty treats before I came here to the woods to help you journey back.

My heart is broken, though I know that we will meet again one day.
My love for you is deeper than my simple words can ever say.
If you do not come by morning I will go and place some flowers on your grave.
Then I will carry on as best I can and try once more to be the one you saw as strong and brave.

Patrick W Kavanagh
28/10/2017

WALK WITH ME

Leave your nagging doubts behind and walk with me to find some quiet place.
When the glamour of the life you thought you'd love has gone.
When the worries and the stresses get too much.
When you've gone along the road as far as you can go
When you learned to doubts the things that used to mean so much.
Then walk with me.

Leave the glaring lights and all the noise behind,
Leave your watch at home and leave your mobile phone.
Walk away from all the sorrows which confuse your weary mind
Find a place where you can truly be alone,
And find me waiting there.

Forest, field or quiet garden.
Beach or park, or just a candle in a quiet room
You will find me in the silence,
Stop and listen, Find the light behind the gloom,
And you will find me there.

You wonder who I am.
I am the gentle touch upon your hair.
I am the comfort and companionship when there is no one there.
I am the eagle flying high, I am the wolf, I am the bear.
I am the Dawning and the End of Time.
Look within yourself, and I am always there.

Patrick W Kavanagh
21/09/2013

ALL HALLOWS EVE

The scratching on the kitchen door, the tapping on the window pane,
The sound of scuffling in the yard, the footsteps running down the lane,
It must be children at their pranks, you close your book and smile and shake your head,
It's almost midnight, time to snuff the candle out and rest your weary head.

The creaking of the wooden stairs is almost deafening as you slowly climb,
You make a promise to repair them for the thousandth time,
And yet another of your many idle, ill-used days have passed,
This job could stay undone, for all you know, this night may be your very last.

The crumpled sheets feel cold and damp, the ancient mattress squeals and groans,
Its rusty springs can barely take the weight of your old creaky bones,
The grimy fireplace long unlit, A dusty mirror that reflects the gloom,
The little, cobwebbed window scarcely lets the light in from the moon.

No bed-time prayers, for prayers have long ceased to mumble from your lips,
Too many losses, to which, a broken heart could never get to grips,
Just one long sigh, perhaps a silent wish to die, you close your weary eyes,
And through the cracked and dusty window, the moon looks down in pity from the skies.

And if you slept and dreamt what happened next, the mortal world will never know,
You saw the spectre of your long-lost love in shining robes as white as snow,
She took your hand and led you to a place with sunlit trees and flowers in bloom,
Your cast-off shell was left behind, - a smiling face amongst the gloom.

FEATHERS

I did not keep the feather that you sent to me today.
I held it up to Father Sky and watched him carry you away.
For far too long, my grief has kept you tethered to my side.
And now, the time has come for you to leave and I to bide.

You were my only friend when friends were difficult to find.
You took the sadness from my heart and all the troubles from my mind.
You gave me all of you and never tallied up the cost.
Then from far beyond the veil, - you came to me again when I was lost.

The little robin came again today, - this time to say goodbye.
I watched her fly away and disappear into the misty sky.
There was a ghostly silence, but I did not feel alone.
You left me in the loving care of her who'll lead me home.

Maybe I can live again, - now that you're far away.
Perhaps I'll wake up to a world where sadness holds no sway.
Perhaps my heart will heal enough to give a love that's equal to the love that I have gained.
Perhaps I'll wake up on that morning feeling glad that I remained.

Patrick W Kavanagh
18/10/2017

DREAMING OF YOU

Do you dream or are you more awake than when I held your hand?
Hand in hand, we walked for many years and shared our laughter and our tears.
Some were tears of joy, for I was blessed to find a heart who understands.
And, now I understand the things you tried to teach me, - though it's taken many years.

For life and death, alike, are simply dreams,
And only when the dreamers wake,
Will we begin to understand exactly what it means...?

Years have passed and understanding taught me how to face the pain.
Like waves, it washes over me in times of sadness and in times of peace.
The pain which comes from knowing I can never hold your hand again.
But sometimes, you return to me and I can feel your touch upon my face.

And in our dreams, - which mirror all the foolish dreams of life,
The sands of time flow backwards to another world, - another life.
And then, I see you once again, - my friend, my lover and my wife.

I am not sad. I cherish all our memories and all the time we had.
I cherish every bright new day, - for who knows when my time will pass away?
I count my many blessings and the many friends who make my heart feel glad.
I live this dream called life as best I can and welcome each new day.

Sometimes, I feel your touch upon my neck the way you used to do.
A wash of brightest yellow glows before my eyes to tell me that it's you.
And then, your gentle voice reminds me of the things I need to do.

You were always so much wiser than I ever hoped to be.
You healed my broken wings, so I could learn to fly again when you were gone.
You healed my anger and my pain, so I could learn to live again.
But when you left my world was broken, and I did not want to carry on.

I know now, that you led me to another who could teach me how to fly.
I understand the measure of your love, and I no longer ask the reason why.
But I will hold her safely in my heart until the day I die.

Thank you for the many, many happy years.
Thank you for the joys, the playful times and even for the tears.
Thank you for the healing which you brought into my life.
Thank you for the happiness you brought me when you chose to be my wife.

In this dream which we call life, I sometimes dream of you.
But now another shares my dreams and shares my love, the way you used to do.
And we will wander hand in hand and heart to heart,
Until our dreams come true.

Patrick W Kavanagh
15/10/2016

TOMORROW

Tomorrow, I will tell you all those loving words which I forgot to say.
Tomorrow, I will do the things I promised but I've never done.
Tomorrow, I will somehow find the will to find a way.
Tomorrow, I will touch the sky and sweep the clouds away.

Yesterday, I did not know enough. I did not have the strength to see it through.
Yesterday, I was not wise enough to understand the things that I should do.
Yesterday, I wallowed in self-pity and I thought I had it tough.
Yesterday, I tried but now I see, - I did not try enough.

Today, I see it all so clear. My moment of awakening is very, very near.
Today, the voices in my head are kind and wisdom, finally, is mine.
Today, I see beyond my foolish hopes and laugh at all my fears.
Today, I feel much stronger than I ever felt in all those yearning years.

Once upon a time, the world was wonderful, and magic filled the air.
Once upon a time we walked with angels and the songs of faeries filled the fragrant air.
Once upon a time, our life was easy, and the fruits were large and ripe on every single tree.
Once upon a time, the world was just exactly as the world was meant to be.

Someday, all our lives will once again be joyful, meaningful and free.
Someday, we will all become the people which we wish that we could be.
Someday, every man and woman will reach out in love to every star and tree.
Someday, we will be that loving family that we were meant to be.

But for today, while I am waiting for this leaden world to turn to gold.
I think that I may try to help this brave new world unfold.
A little kindness to that stranger in the street, or just a simple smile to everyone I meet.
Finally, I realise this is the moment I must choose my victory or my defeat.

Patrick W Kavanagh
08/10/2017

THE FEAR OF FLYING

Take my hand and I won't let you go.
Leave behind the world which you once thought was all you'd ever know.
Those tragedies that seemed so real, -
Those hurt-filled thoughts which made you reel,
The wounds and scars that you believed would never, ever, heal.

Stretch your new-found wings and glide across the moonlit sky.
The moon herself is not so far away for those who truly yearn to fly.
As the twinkling lights below go past remember you are free at last,
And you may stay, or slip away this very night,
To find a land where all is wonder and delight.

But, isn't she so pretty, underneath the rising moon?
This earth who gave you birth into a life you wish to leave behind so soon.
You might want to dally just a little longer, - there are many things you may still want to do.
But you may go or you may leave, -
The choice is left entirely up to you.

There is so much pain in life, - this much is very true.
There are duties and commitments and unpleasant things to do.
But, also, there is laughter and companionship and even sometimes, bliss.
I wonder if you're ready yet to leave behind a world like this.
I wonder if you're certain there is nothing that you'll miss.

Come and rest your sleepy head upon my loving breast.
A little sleep, perhaps, is all you need to put your miseries to rest.
Let us fly, in dreams, beyond the forests and the fields and high above the sparkling streams.
A new perspective on the world may heal your wounds and ease those aches and pains,
And in the morning, you will wake renewed, refreshed, to face the world again.

ON A STARRY NIGHT

The world is resting from a long and sunny day.
A hint of summers calming breeze has chased the wispy clouds away.
I sit and gaze across the ripened fields and sleepy trees,
That gently sway and flutter to the wind with lazy leaves.

The yellow moon is looking down. Her smile is warm and bright.
Her love is giving gentle light to guard her children in the night.
Only laughter is allowed in all the worlds to which her children fly.
When in their dreams they travel to the lands beyond the sky.

Swirling colours dance and glide across imaginations eyes.
Painting all the colours of the rainbow on the starry skies.
The dreamers dream and night-time sparkles high above our sleepy heads.
When the children are all safely tucked up in their beds.

Patrick W Kavanagh.
1/10/2017

WHEN I AM ALONE

When my sadness tells me that there's nothing left inside.
When life has lost its joy and all I want to do is run and hide.
When bitterness and sorrow poison everything I do.
The one remaining comfort in my lonely life is you.

I walk the quiet streets and I can feel you everywhere.
I feel your gentle presence in the cool night breeze that lays a kiss upon my hair
I hear you in the rustle of the Autumn leaves that swirl around me as I walk.
You listen to my every word when, finally, I find the will to talk.

Who but you can lead me safely home when I am lost?
Who is always there to rescue me and never counts the cost?
You are the one who answers every question if I only listen to the things you have to say.
You are there when sleep has fled and all I have is dread-filled thoughts about the coming days.

When you have raised my spirits high you share in all my joys.
You are the warmth of Summer's sun, - the shimmering blue in Summers sunny skies.
You are the Way, the Truth and all of Life. You are the love that sparkles in a stranger's eyes.
You are the tongue which always speaks the truth, - the tongue that never lies.

There is nothing I must do to please you, - but to feel you I must resonate your love.
It is written in the stars that everything I do below reflects in all the worlds above.
Your wisdom, deep inside me, tells me that I must become the world I wish to see.
Your patience tells me, that if I should fail a thousand times,
Your love still waits for me.

WHEN YOU AND I WERE ONE

When you and I were one.
Our love was an unbroken chain of bliss before the world began.
That chain was stretched until our hearts were torn when first the earth was born
But, still, the bond of love between us like a thousand rivers ran.

Love flowed into being as the water from a million mountain springs.
I reached out to you from deep within the void to share the essence of my being.
I those days my ancient heart rejoiced to hear your voices ring.
Your voices reaching out to me became the songs which choirs of angels sing.

Lift your heart to mine again and let us share our love again.
Your darkness casts a poisoned dart into my grieving heart and dims my loving light.
I, - your father and your mother and your sister and your friend,
Cannot bear the silence of your absence, or the sorrow of your self-inflicted night.

When times are hard, I hear your call, - I feel you flinch with every ache and pain.
When life is good, I dance for joy with you beneath the Summer rain.
Come to me once more and bring to me, your peace and love and joy,
Touch me once again through all the many multi-coloured threads which join the world,
Then, you and I can be as one again.

Patrick W Kavanagh
24/09/2017

WHO LISTENS?

Who will listen on that day when I can stand this life no more?
Who will send that little boat to take me safely to the other shore?
When my fears and all my tears have worn away my love for life.
Who will take me to that place beyond all pain and strife?

Sometimes, I can feel you standing near me, - 'though I do not know your name.
On those happy days, - Your presence keeps me warm and safe through snow and wind and rain.
On blessed days like this, a single flower may bring me to the edge of bliss.
And just a touch of summer wind against my cheek feels like an angel's kiss.

I remember you from long ago when I was just a child.
You never seemed to care that I was ragged, poor and wild.
You never stood in judgement of my hand-me-downs and sullen frowns.
And when I screamed in rage, I felt your calming touch when there was no one else around.

Then a world of doubt crept in and so, the dark nights of my soul began.
I searched for you in every hidden place but could not find you anywhere I ran.
Those empty, restless years when no one else could soothe the pain of losing you.
Those years when nothing filled that yawning void, - no matter what I tried to do.

Then one day I laid my burdens on the stony ground and wept until my tears had all run dry.
Bereft of hope and gone beyond all pain I simply turned to look up at the sky.
Angels graced the soft white clouds and graceful dragons flew behind.

And when I saw the faeries dance around me then I knew I'd lost my mind.
Who would cherish sanity when madness brings such bliss?
Who would choose a life of avarice and grime above an angel's kiss?
Somehow, I have found once more what I had thought was lost for evermore.
And I will cherish every moment of this new-found life until I find that other shore.

Patrick W Kavanagh
17/09/2017

I REMEMBER YOU

I remember you.
You stood beside me once and swore that, for forever, you'd be mine.
I remember you.
I feel that I have walked beside you for the longest time.
I remember you.
Your eyes have lost that lustre and your hair is turning grey.
I remember you.
You lied to me that day you promised that you'd never go away.

I remember you.
You tucked me into bed each night and said that everything would be all right.
I remember you.
You were always there to soothe my cares when nightmares frightened in the night.
I remember you.
You built a wall of love around my world and kept me safe from harm in every way you could.
I remember you.
And I would find you once again If only there was some way that I could.

We remember you.
We had a birthday party yesterday and even brought some candles and a cake.
We remember you.
As we watched you try to blow those tiny candles out we thought our hearts would break.
We remember you.
And we remember and all the strength and beauty which you brought into our lives.
We remember you.
And now we feel so lost each time we see the sadness and confusion in your eyes.

We remember all the long and happy years.
There was joy enough in life to soothe the hurt and dry away the tears.
Although your body and your mind are broken, - deep inside your spirit's waiting patiently to fly.
And we will cherish every moment still remaining to be shared.
Until the moment comes when we must briefly say goodbye.

Patrick W Kavanagh
16/09/2017

THE HEALER'S LAMENT

I wish I had some clever words or secret spell to take the pain away.
But you and I both know the world just simply doesn't work that way.
We both can soothe and heal with all the energy which Spirit and which Nature may imbue.
But the demons which live deep within the soul of Man are not so easy to subdue.

Fear is chief among them and with just a whisper in our ear he fills our world with dread.
Then he fills our hearts with anguish as he chants his mantras of destruction in our heads.
Those tales of horror which were placed within us when we were too young to realise,
That, if we really want to fly then all we need to do is look up at the skies.

The past is gone, but still, its long and heavy chains are dragging us behind.
The rattle of those bulky iron links drives love and beauty from our minds.
Its sticky web of dark defeat entraps us as it wraps around our stumbling feet.
If only we would let our wings unfurl, - then we could leave behind those dull and dreary streets.

Those alleyways which lead our troubled minds astray and wander through our past.
Could once again become the shadows underneath our wings as we fly nimbly past.
We have no need to sit and wallow in our dark despair so filled with woes and pain.
When Spirit stands beside us and can lift us high above Fears dark and cavernous domain.

Patrick W Kavanagh
06/09/2017

THE LONG GOODBYE

So many loving years, - so many smiles and, now and then, some tears,
Those many joys we shared throughout the happy years.
These memories we shared will never fade from me.
Although sometimes, you peer at me in dazed uncertainty

Our memories are written on my heart on plates of gold,
They will never slip away or fade as I grow old.
Each day, I softly call your name and hold your hand and smile,
and try to be your memory, for just a while

I dread the moments when the light of recognition fails,
It makes me feel that I am all alone, - it makes you look so frail,
My life becomes a prison guard's, - your happy home becomes a jail,
But I will always try to light the love-light in your eyes however often I may fail.

You have not passed away from me and I can never say goodbye.
Sometimes, I see your face, as if another wears your skin and cannot grasp just why.
I see a frightened child where once I saw my love, my life, my kin,
and, it's so hard to see you there before me when you will not let me in.

This broken body that was yours is all that I have left, of all that I held dear,
But you are there my love, behind the panic and confusion and the fear.
Be still my love, be calm, for time is fleeting in this vale of tears,
And soon our spirits both will rise and cast away the troubled years,
and we shall be as one again someday.

Patrick W Kavanagh
19/05/2013

LOOKING BACK

Ah! Such wisdom I have sought.
I searched for it in every pompous and opinionated book I ever bought.
I must admit that I've been fooled by clever words when I was young.
But wisdom finally appears with age when all our cleverness is done.

Our wisdom comes from aches and pains which we began to notice when our lives were almost done.
Our wrinkled weathered skins remind us of our many days of rain and wind and sun.
We can look back in amazement at how clever we once were.
In those days when we were legends in our foolish minds and lived without a care.

Finally, I understand the looks that elders gave when I propounded each new theory as the ultimate design.
We felt that all the world was ours to take and all we needed was a little time.
But time flows on without a second thought while many hours are worked for every item bought.
And then we looked around and realised our lives were spent and gone without a second thought.

Now that we are growing old and we are learning to be truly wise.
We gaze with just a little sadness at the beauty of the evening skies.
All that beauty soon will be a legacy that we have handed down to those we leave behind.
And all the wisdom we have gained will once again be treasure for another soul to find.

Perhaps it's just the way this crazy world was meant to be.
A school where every generation must create a brand-new history.
Perhaps we take our wisdom with us and its memory upon this world is lost.
So those who come behind must choose a brand-new path and pay what it may cost.

RUNNING AWAY

Wherever you may go becomes exactly where you are.
Even if you travel to the furthest, brightest star.
You lock your doors, - you shut your blinds and stay indoors instead.
But still, you cannot hush the droning voices in your head.

In the end, you will accept yourself for just exactly who you are.
In the end, you'll realise that every man and every woman is a fool.
Eternity is waiting, it is always just within your reach.
The deity within you uses life to mock and goad and teach.

The day will come when you will laugh at all of this.
The fight for wealth, the yearning for respect, the longing for a lover's kiss.
A morning soon will come when you will wake to see it's just a game.
Then, you will smile with kindness in the mirror and you'll never be the same.

Sometimes I see it clearly, but sometimes the vision fades.
Yet I know that those who do not live in love are living in a self-made Hell.
It is such an easy rule to learn but many of us fail.
Each time you judge another, - you will judge yourself as well.

Kindness is the only way to live a better life and forge a better day.
Understanding helps. It opens us to learn from others how to find a better way.
The person you despise may simply be a victim of your unexamined lies.
The person whom you fear may hold the truth you badly need to hear.

Sit and breathe and simply be.
The person who you think you are will die, but there will always be a "Me"
That voiceless presence deep within who guides you, - if you simply ask.
There are no preparations needed nor some pointless futile tasks.

"You are gods!" the prophet said, - yet none of them could understand.
They prayed and fasted, and they gazed up at the stars, but all they had to do was take his hand.
Find the wisdom in each blade of grass and every leaf and stone.
In the stillness of your search, you'll find your way back home.

Patrick W Kavanagh
19/08/2017

JUST FOR TODAY

Just for today, I am resolved to listen to the trees.
Even here within this room, I hear them whisper in the breeze.
They speak of Summer's now long past.
They tell me that the song of life will last.
But now the time has come to settle into Winter's gentle peace.

Even now, the leaves are swirling 'round the windowpane.
They called to say goodbye and promise that they will be back again.
I softly sigh a sweet goodbye
To all of Summer's passing Joys.
And gaze out at the leaden skies which soon will bring the rain.

Suddenly, my eyes are dazzled as the Autumn sun bursts through the clouded sky.
I feel as if Persephone, herself, has called to say goodbye.
Osiris lights the world with sparkling reds and golds.
As if to set a fitting tableau for his lover to behold.
And Hades waits with bated breath to witness, once again, his rivals death.

Just for today, I am determined to accept each moment as it flows.
Just like the past, the future is a dream, and where we will awaken,- no one knows.
The wheel of life will turn and, soon enough, the Beltane fires will burn.
And I will keep the warmth of Summer in my heart until my love returns.
With all the beauty and the joy for which the Winter yearns.

Patrick W Kavanagh
31/10/2016

ANGELS BORN SLEEPING

I am sorry that my passing caused you so much heartache and such pain.
Although my sleeping form looks still and cold, - I am reborn again.
A higher call has summoned me to worlds beyond your sight.
And I am in a place of love and wonder, - and delight.

I will visit often, though you may not know that I am near.
But, if you listen carefully, who knows what you may hear.
My quiet voice will whisper words of comfort and of love,
For I have had the grace of being chosen by the one above.

Your sacrifice and sorrow will have never been in vain.
For our spirit lives forever and we all will meet again.
But I must be a messenger of hope and love to many who are born.
For I am now a light, to all who wait in darkness, for a bright new dawn.

Do not grieve too long for me or shed too many tears.
For I have risen far above all grief and left behind all sorrows and all fears.
I know you wished to be my guide and my protector and to share in all my joys.
But, soon enough, we'll meet again beyond the starry skies.

Patrick W Kavanagh.
16/10/2016

SIAN

I know your spirit hears me,
I feel that, deep within, you understand the meaning of my love.
Although your body struggles to respond, -
From far beyond the chains of broken dreams I hear you call.

You are innocence, - a pure, untarnished spirit
Loosely tethered to this world by tangled cords.
I feel the deep and lasting bond between us,
Even though capricious Nature stole away your words.

I will not forsake you to the fitful care of others for as long as strength allows.
I will be the guardian of your dreams when I am bent and bowed.
And I will not be broken by the twisted logic of their senseless laws.
For you were sent to me so we could be the best that life allows.

Patrick W Kavanagh
11/01/2017

SMILE

Smile!
We understand your broken heart.
We cannot bear your tears.
You've cried for far too many years,
But still, the sadness burns your eyes so much,
You dare not look up to the skies.
So, smile.

Smile!
Find someone more broken than you feel.
Reaching out to them may heal your broken heart.
But anyway, it goes, - at least it is a start.
Your tears have failed to wash away the pain.
Perhaps the time has come for dancing in the rain?
So, smile.

Smile!
Life is never easy, - but only you can make it dull.
Only you can make empty, - only you can make it full.
Life was never meant to be a dream.
And, even if it was, the dreamer must decide exactly what it means,
Or, maybe you can just awaken to a bright new dawn?
So, Smile.

Smile!
Our time is short, and time for those we love, - is shorter still.
Grief will come, and we cannot evade that bitter pill.
Soon enough our world will end, -
With no time left to make amends.
Barely time enough for love and making friends.
So, smile.

Patrick William Kavanagh
01/10/2016

WHO WILL CRY FOR ME

Who will cry for me when I am gone?
Who will sit beside my sleeping form until my final dawn?
Who will see the beauty in the life I tried to live?
Who will see the worth of all the gifts I tried to give?
And who will spend a moment just to come and say goodbye,
When my weary soul is free at last to fly?

Do not ask me to apologise for any harm you feel I've done.
Do not pick my tattered corpse for any profit, - as I'm sure there will be none.
Do not ask me to forgive you for imagined wrongs that have been done.
I promise you that they were all forgiven long before the setting sun.
And as my sun is sinking deep into that vast eternal sea,
The only thing I ask is that you say goodbye and let me be.

Death has never given me a single cause to fear.
Death is just a doorway to the things which I hold dear.
Far beyond that distant night, - are worlds of wonder and delight,
And I shall keep the ones I love forever in my sight.
So, do not weep too hard or mourn too long,
For I will not be very far away, - if you should need my love when I am gone.

Live every single moment just as if it were your very last.
Trust me when I say that life is fleeting, and the time goes quickly past.
Oh! To have another hundred years with all its pain and hardship and its tears.
But the time has passed so quickly while I slept through all the many wasted years.
And now I find that I must go, and leave so many things undone,
And start again, afresh, beneath a very different sun.

I want to leave you some advice before I go away.
Ask the universe for just a single joyful day.
Then ask again tomorrow if by chance you should awake,
And add a plea for courage, - for the risks you need to take.
Live your life as fully as you can, and smile with gratitude for every single breath.
Then you will never need to fear that enigmatic doorway, - we call death.

Patrick W Kavanagh
16/09/2016

FINALLY, YOU CAME

Finally, you came.
Gathering light and laughter
after Summers gentle rain.

Childhood follows you.
A gift to all who learn to see
The world as it was meant to be.

Only tears of joy may fall,
When by innocence,
We are enthralled.

Laughter is the only sound,
Which can be heard today.
When lost within your sway.

Beauty is the only sight.
Our hearts are filled with pure delight,
When you are near.

Patrick W Kavanagh
14/08/2016

WALK WITH ME

Leave your nagging doubts behind and walk with me to find some quiet place.
When the glamour of the life you thought you'd love has gone.
When the worries and the stresses get too much.
When you've gone along the road as far as you can go
When you learned to doubts the things that used to mean so much.
Then walk with me.

Leave the glaring lights and all the noise behind,
Leave your watch at home and leave your mobile phone.
Walk away from all the sorrows which confuse your weary mind
Find a place where you can truly be alone,
And find me waiting there.

Forest, field or quiet garden.
Beach or park, or just a candle in a quiet room
You will find me in the silence,
Stop and listen, Find the light behind the gloom,
And you will find me there.

You wonder who I am.
I am the gentle touch upon your hair.
I am the comfort and companionship when there is no one there.
I am the eagle flying high, I am the wolf, I am the bear.
I am the Dawning and the End of Time.
Look within yourself, and I am always there.

Patrick W Kavanagh
21/09/2013

LIFE IS SWEET

Life is sweet, like honeyed mead that dallies on the tongue.
Yet scarce a day has passed that I've not wondered where you've gone.
Even as a naïve youth, - your haunting eyes disturbed my dreams.
But they were depths which I was ill-equipped to probe, and so,
I chose to try to make you laugh by any foolish means.

I loved you deeply in my ill-considered, clumsy, childish way.
I could not face the sorrow in your eyes, I am ashamed to say.
I doubt I could have ever understood enough to ease your pain.
My thoughts were filled with love and laughter, like a shallow stream.
But now I feel the touch of sadness, - knowing you will never come again.

Where did you go, - that you should disappear so suddenly without a trace?
What shall I do, - now that I realise that I will never see again, - that haunting face?
Did you travel to the western isles where every heart is freed from loves cruel guile?
Or did you simply fade away into the distant past from whence you came?
There is no trace of you and I have travelled many, many roads and wandered many miles.

Many are the lips I kissed but none so sweet as when I first kissed you.
Finest wines and brandies I have supped but none as sweet as when we sipped the morning dew.
I have had a happy life, - but you always kept a corner of my eye, in case you came.
Many a young maiden caught my second glance, - due to a passing semblance to your frame.
But now I feel so very certain that you'll never come again.

I cannot tell for certain through the lashing rain which stings my eyes.
I think I see your silhouette against the leaden clouds that drench the thunderous skies.
I think I may be laughing once again, but everything is deafened by the rattling, raging storm.
I think I may be running, but I cannot feel the shifting, muddy ground beneath my feet.
My heart is reaching out to you, - I will not concede defeat.

Finally, we touch, and salty tears are merged on rain-soaked lips.
A lifetimes loss is swept away in just a single interval of bliss.
Hand in hand we walk into the wind-whipped forest where the trees are tossed and torn.
There is no need for words for I am by your side and all I was is now reborn.
I feel your arms around me and I am content to sleep in your embrace until the coming morn.

Patrick W Kavanagh
12/08/2016

DANCING IN THE RAIN

I stood entranced as silver pearls cascaded from your long blond hair.
You swirled in tireless circles as you scattered raindrops everywhere.
Mesmerised, I stood and gazed as sundown set the watery sky ablaze.
I watched you dancing in the rain one Summer's evening, and my life will never be the same.

Without you, the moon would be a dusty ball of rock that slowly spins in space.
And all my life would be a lonely drudge, bereft of hope or joy or grace.
The beauty of your violet eyes transcends the bluest of the Summers skies.
If you were gone, I would forever crave the coldest comfort of a single kiss goodbye.

I close my eyes and see the rivulets of water running down your breasts and thighs.
I see, once more, the gentle summer rain pours down from almost empty skies.
The patter of the raindrops on the nearby trees brings such a sense of peace and ease.
My naked feet caress the meadow flowers as the gentle shower is swept along by Summer's breeze.

Life has no greater charm than walking arm in arm, while subtle glances hold the promise of a kiss.
There is no greater bliss than that first taste of sweetness from a charming lovers' lips.
There is no greater joy than dreaming that we'll always be together, - you and I.
And I will love you always, though our Summer days may slip away, and all our years fly by.

Patrick W Kavanagh
23/07/2016

BABES IN THE WOOD

We never realised that we were only babes lost in the woods;
Playing hide and seek, - while silently the world moved on.
We wished and dreamed, that always, was a faithful world;
But while we dreamed our dreams, forever slipped away
And I woke up to find my world was gone.

I love another now, but that will never change my love for you.
She healed my heart and brought back from summer's open door.
I learned to live somehow and carried on; - as lovers sometimes do.
And now we live a life that I had never dreamed of when we wandered in the woods,
And I can never change back to that person, whom I was before.

Springtime aches, - where once it brought a joyfulness to every step.
And yet there is gratitude within my heart for all of Spirits gifts.
I know that you are watching over me; - I know that you still care.
I looked into your eyes the other week and saw the love still there.
Although they graced another's face, my heart still knew that it was truly you.

I want to tell you all about the love whom I have found,
But, I guess you know already, as you often hang around.
She has the bluest, deepest eyes that I have ever seen.
She's pretty as a picture, - with the kindest heart that there has ever been.
Without her love and strength, - I do not know how life could possibly have been.

I'll say goodbye, - although I know that you are never very far away.
I listened carefully to every word you said, - I promise I will cherish every day.
I know that life is much too short to waste in misery and in despair,
And I will try to wake up every day and look at life for all the blessings there.
I will go and live my life and leave regret behind,
But please forgive me if, I sometimes shed a tear,
When life's lost blessings slip into my mind.

Patrick W Kavanagh
13/03/2016

I REMEMBER ME

I remember me,
Suddenly, as plain as plain can be,
I see the world as clear as childlike eyes can see,
and I am young once more.

Once more. I see the world is fresh and new,
and filled with wonder and amazing things to do.
Spider webs that sparkle with the sunlit dew,
and I am young once more.

The colours of the garden fill my eyes,
Cool green grass, the warm sun flashing rainbows in my eyes,
The fluffy clouds that drift across the pale blue skies,
and I am young once more.

What shall I do with this; - my rediscovered youth,
Shall I find a net and hunt for butterflies or newts,
Or shall I sit here in my quiet place, - it matters not,
for I am young once more.

I remember me,
And all I ever was is here; - All in life that I held dear,
All that I have ever shared in love has never left,
And I can see it all so clearly now,
And I am young once more.

Patrick W Kavanagh
03/03/13

LOVERS MOON

Dance with me once more beneath the sleepy moon.
The dawn begins to peek above the purple mountains all too soon.
The night has passed too quickly, and the garish daylight looms.
For me, without your smile, - the brightest day brings nought but gloom.

Whisper to me, one more time, - of love that never dies.
Show me once again, that far off world beneath the violet skies.
Share another kiss for all the ones which soon I'll miss.
For there is nothing left in life, for me, - but this.

Many were the nights I lay alone, by choice, before we met.
My heart was made of stone, and would still be, - if we were strangers yet.
But not a heart exists which can resist a faeries kiss,
And now my heart beats just for you alone, and none can query this.

How can I go back to dusty books when I have lain with you in quiet nooks?
Or tread the beaten path when I have walked the misty, moonlit road past sparkling brooks.
My weary eyes despise the bored and foppish dress of clerks,
When I have gazed upon the shining diamonds of your eyes, in caverns deep and dark.

Take my life, before you go away and break my foolish love-struck heart in two.
Do not leave this hollow husk behind with nothing left but memories of you.
Have pity on this mortal man.
And love me for whatever years are left in human life's short span.
Take me to the world which blossomed long before the world of man began.

Patrick W Kavanagh
23/02/2016

I SHOULD BE GONE

I should be gone,
Away across the fields and rolling hills,
Away to sit by noisy little mountain streams,
Away to where my soul can dream its dreams,
Away to where my heart can drink its fill.
And God and I can be as one.
I should be gone.

I should be gone,
To where my naked feet can feel the rustling leaves upon the forest floor,
To where the air is cool and moist, and spirit moves with every breath,
To where I can face equally the thought of life and death,
To where it's easier to see, they are both one, and we can live forever more.
And Goddess holds my hand and we can be as One.
I should be gone

I should be gone,
Across the oceans wide and dark and deep,
Across to where a stony solitary keep protects my will.
Across the Planets, moving oh so silent and so still
Across the Universe, into the great uncharted depths of space.
Across to where I seek that Sacred Place
To where I seek a special Grace,
I should be gone.

I should be gone,
Beyond the bounds of what we foolishly mistake as real.
Beyond the chains that make us think this life is all, we have,
Beyond this fleeting world that flows away so fast,
Beyond the limitations that we set on what we feel,
To where the universe and I are one.
To where the Truth is finally revealed.
I Should Be Gone.

AWAY FOR CHRISTMAS

The Christmas tree lights up, - but you are gone so very far away
And yet, somehow, I feel your hand, so softly clasping mine.
I catch your fragrance in the air and know that you are near.
And feel the warmth of memories that come so fresh and clear,

I sense your presence, though my heart is aching, and my tears will burn,
And as we place the presents underneath the tree, I hold a certainty inside, that someday, somehow you will finally return.
I will put away all thoughts of sadness, for the sake of those whom I hold dear.
For, even in our darkest hour, there is a Light that shines with love for those for whom we care.

Hearts that love the way we love can never really be apart,
Hearts that hope beyond all hope will have their hopes fulfilled one day.
This has always been love's law and this has always been love's way.
And I will wait, until my waiting days, and all my waiting years, have passed away.

I will hold you safe within my heart, and we will meet again,
I know that this is true, although I may not know for certain, when.
May you rest in Summer-land until our hearts are healed.
And I will hold you in my arms one day when life's true beauty is revealed.

Patrick W Kavanagh
19/12/2015.

ANGELS IN THE WIND

I stand and feel the wind's embrace as kisses, soft as feathers, touch my smiling face.
Gentle laughter, hushed as falling snow is calling, - and it leads me where I need to go.
Swirling leaves are blowing all around, -that somehow leave a gleaming trace.
But as the seasons meet within my heart, I feel a joy, an all-consuming grace.

It grieves me little now to say that all I think I know will, someday, pass away.
It does not matter that the world will turn, and all my dreams may die and never be reborn.
This perfect moment is enough, within the pause between the night time and the day.
With tiny angels dancing all around in laughter and in play.

"Walk with us between the worlds and let imagination fly.
We will show that all who ever lived, will never die.
We will heal your aching heart and help you understand,
That only love can heal the world and soothe the heart of man."

Patrick W Kavanagh
16/11/2015

MY BELOVED

I stand before the gods and swear that each of us has honoured every pledge.
The gilded cage that kept you safe and warm became a prison when your wings were fully fledged.
Perhaps the time is past for us to journey side by side, - the gate is open, and the keeper stands aside.
The time has come to fly away and seek those bright blue skies reflected in your violet eyes.

When my love for life had drained away you came and filled my heart with yours.
You came and gave me hope and comfort in those dark and lonely wretched hours.
You have been my guide, my angel and my trusted friend who healed my broken heart.
But there are wounds which never truly heal and tear the truest loves apart.

We are peaceful warriors in this battleground which many foolishly believe is all of life.
We will walk the web which Spirit weaves though it may lead through suffering and strife.
My heart is always yours and none can doubt our fate will be forever intertwined.
I know it in my soul that every friend will have my blessing and each enemy of yours will be forever mine.

Patrick W Kavanagh
18/06/2017

THANK YOU FOR THE FLOWERS

Thank you for the flowers,
Although I always liked to see them sparkling in the Summer rain.
Still, I hope they bring you comfort in this time of grief and pain.

I came to say, - I miss you just as much as I know you miss me.
This world I have inherited in such a sad untimely way is just a different way of being free.
And things are very different here although I still remember who you used to know as me.

I understand your need to cry,
But raise your head for me, so I can see the clear blue sky.
I long to lay once more beside the breezy shores and watch the little clouds go scudding by.

Take a walk for me along a warm and sunny beach so I can feel the sand beneath my feet once more.
And know that I am not unhappy as there's so much here to learn and to explore.
But still, a tiny part of me is longing just to touch your face once more.

Patrick W Kavanagh
06/06/2017

WE WILL RISE

We may rise just like the eagle who commands the clear blue skies.
We may rise just like the sparrow as the eagle's shadow falls across his frightened eyes.
We may rise just like the morning sun to cast our light on all with eyes to see.
But we will rise to face each bright new day and be the best that we can be.

We may fall a thousand times each gifted, sacred day.
We may fail to see the wonder and the magic as we stumble on our way.
We may fill each night with bitter tears and useless longing for the half-forgotten years.
But we will rise again each morning as we face once more our sadness and our fears.

We are stronger than the bright and burning steels which heroes forged into the sharpest swords when evil came with fangs and claws.
We are wiser than the sages and the wisest princes who pronounced our ancient sacred laws.
We are brighter than the sun, which soon enough will cool, but even now cannot outshine our spirits vast eternal light.
Our dreams are softer and more gentle than the wistful moon which guides the traveller through this fleeting night.

We will rise one day to see that there never really was an 'us and them' or 'you and me.'
We will rise one day and realise that we already are the people whom we always wished to be.
We will rise to see acceptance eases every wound and kindness brings us every worthwhile answer to be found.
We will rise and build a world of peace and fairness where each creature whispers words of love with many different sounds.

Patrick W Kavanagh
27/05/2017

ASHES IN THE WIND

I watch them fly,
Biting winds bring streaming tears to red-rimmed eyes,
Air so cold, it creeps into the bones and chills the very soul,
Where will they go,
These ashes in the wind.

Flesh and blood reduced to memories,
Purified amidst a fiery blaze,
And as they fly, - we wonder why?
We wonder what we'll do?
When all that we once loved,
Are ashes in the wind.

The flesh is gone,
The Spirit is revealed,
Like a beacon for the blind,
Like a symphony for those who cannot hear.
Like the fragrance of a rose outside a shuttered window.
Those who go before us leave us signs,
But all that we can see,
Are ashes in the wind.

Patrick W Kavanagh
30/01/13

THE PASSING

Let me lie in the sunshine with clear blue skies.
I will gaze at the hills where the eagle flies.
Her strong wings will carry me far away,
To a land where the night has surrendered to day.

Do not weep at my passing, my time here was done.
I go now, to dance and to sing to the sun.
The butterflies call me with voices so still,
I will fly with the eagle wherever she wills.

My life was a rainbow, my work was just play,
I never loved night-time, my time was the day.
My journey's not over, - it's only begun.
I go to a new life beneath a bright sun.

Please don't blame the poet for this childish rhyme.
I need him to tell you it was just my time.
I came here to visit, - it wasn't for long.
Now I laugh in the sunlight and sing a new song.

Patrick W Kavanagh
14/11/2015

THE FINAL DUSK

I fill my glass with golden light, -
Capturing the memories of twenty thousand dusks.
To the almost empty goblet of my life,
I add this final sunset and the end of all my tasks.
I do not crave my three score years and ten, -
This is the perfect moment for my less than perfect life to end.

I have no regrets.
I have done the things my heart has always craved to do.
Now the time has come to slip away.
My fleeting form will vanish with the rising sun,
Just like the morning dew.
And, gladly though I go, - I will cherish every moment that I spent with you.

Do not bore your gods with prayers on my behalf.
Do not make my passing dreary with your laments and your tears.
Raise your glasses and your voices, -
Send me on my way with songs and with a laugh.
If I meet your gods upon my journey, -
I will surely plead on your behalf!

Life is just a passing dream.
Death is just a brief awakening in the middle of the night.
Nothing in this world is real enough to justify your anguish or your fright.
So, laugh and play each day away,
Until the moment comes when you must fight, -
Then stand your ground and strike with all your might.

We are warriors and priests.
We were never meant to live our lives like sheep.
We have no right to stand around and bleat
While one by one we all get rounded up and fleeced.
Security is just another fancy word for fear.
The time has come to shout so loud that even those within the highest towers will hear.

Patrick W Kavanagh
02/08/2017

WHISPERS IN THE WIND

Did I hear you in the muted whispers of the wind?
Did I feel you softly touch each tingling strand of hair?
Something deep within my heart assures me that you are my one true kin.
You, - who are the promise of the Spring when Winter's storms move in.
You who spin the web I call my life and weave the magic in.

I am not your servant nor your master,
We are simply strands of energy which span that great imaginary void.
I can make no claim to greater wisdom than the rest,
I have simply walked that solitary path which many folks avoid.
And found, for every challenge which it brings I find one hundred other ways in which I have been blessed.

You cannot forsake me, - I am yours and you are mine.
And though I may forget you, - you are part of every fibre of my being.
You are woven into all I do and part of all I am, - both human and divine.
You are my lover and my teacher and my guide to realms unseen.
Your kisses taste like honey and your lips are like the sweetest, reddest wine.

Patrick W Kavanagh
22/07/2017

BEYOND THE RAGGED FIELDS

Beyond the ragged fields with crumbling dry-stone walls, we walked, - as lovers often do.
The drunken farmer slept, as quietly beyond his beggared boundaries we crept.
Beneath her long black dress, her snow-white feet were bathed by the morning dew.
Her heart was mine, - her beauty was divine,
And yet, the secrets of her long black garb no lover ever knew.

Ah! Sweet Eileen, I would die for just one kiss from your sweet lips.
No rouge has ever stained the softness which my eyes alone have managed to caress.
I cannot win your father's grace with gifts or land or gold,
For fortune has not shone upon this travelling man though I am brave and bold.
I have fought in many wars but now my horse and gun have long been sold.

If I could find Fitzgibbon, - he's a colonel in the army and one day I saved his life.
I am sure his gratitude would set me up so I could ask for you to be my wife.
But he is many miles away and long before I could return, I fear that you'll be wed.
And I would pluck the eyes from my own head before I'd see you in another's bed.
Although I've lived through many wars, without you by my side I may as well be dead.

Come with me across the sea to where a man and woman can live free.
There are lands and plenty for the brave who dare to risk the tempests and the waves.
I'll take the shilling one more time if you will promise to be mine.
And then, our passage will be paid to find our fortune far across the sea.
Where we can start a family and build a bright new life for you and me.

Her eyes were all that gave reply as on they walked beneath a misty sky.
She slipped her hand in his as morning mist became a blanket of the softest weave.
Stepping blindly forward, they embraced their brave new world,
While all around, the thick white morning fog began to whirl.
And in the little village, all were woken by the ringing of a single bell.

A neighbour saw them walking in the fog,
And shook his head in ancient wisdom as they wandered hand in hand into the bog.
I hope they found their brave new world, - for what became of them no one can tell.
No letter ever came from far away, and not a single word for fifty years.
And every time that church bell rang her father drank a little more to hide his tears.

Patrick W Kavanagh
16/07/2017

OUR SECRET PLACE

You woke me as the twilight slipped into the midnight hours.
Do not think to warm my cold, cold heart with dying flowers.
This unmarked grave which only you and I could ever find.
Is where I lost my life, my love, my hope, my heart and mind.

Did you bury me from guilt? Was I abandoned here in sorrow or in shame?
Why have you left me here in this sad place where no one knows my name?
Do you steal my corpse just as you stole my dreams the day, I took your name?
Once I was the dream of many men, but now those days will never come again.

What have I done that was so wrong that you should strike me down?
Why, in this secret place where once we met as lovers, have you laid me in the ground?
It broke my heart that you had found a sweeter love to warm your bed each night.
Yet, all I asked was that you send your callow love away and try to set things right.

Now the moonlight is the only welcome sight that I will ever see.
I curse the foolish, trusting girl, who once, I used to be.
Stupidly, I loved too much, - My tender heart had fooled my empty head.
Go! Before I drag your screaming carcass down into my ill-made bed.

Patrick W Kavanagh
07/07/2017

THE SILENCE

The silence was always there,
Hidden by the clamour of imaginary needs and false despair.
If I am immortal, then this chance will come again.
If not, then in a few short years my self-inflicted suffering will end.

Do not weep because your childhood dreams have never come to pass.
You are exactly where you chose to be, - just change your script to change your future and your past.
Life is just a fairy-tale which tells the stories and the roles we chose to play.
In the silence we can choose another path, - another way.

When your soul is ready you will find your wings and fly.
Perhaps to find another place within this world or underneath a very different sky.
It matters little where you choose to be.
One day you'll wake to realise that I was always you and you were always me.

Patrick W Kavanagh
20/06/2017

THE PHOENIX

Like a Phoenix, from the ashes of my former life I rise.
Flaming wings that stretch and glow against the starry skies.
Spirit fills me as I leave behind the limitations of my former days.
The wisdom of the ages and beyond are mine, to help me choose the way.

Do not drench my dried-up carcass with your wasted tears.
Do not mourn my passing, after all the wasted years.
I am free at last to leave my bitterness and all my anger and regret behind.
The time has come to search the worlds beyond to see what I may find.

I will fly away to many strange new worlds of which I never even dreamed.
For suddenly the possibilities are so much greater than they ever seemed.
Far across the vast expanse of space. Past the universes, and beyond all time.
And once again to choose a life, that for a little while, I will call mine.

Do not pity me and do not weep.
I simply slipped into another world as I lay fast asleep.
Gone for just a while are all the worries, - all the strain.
Until the day will come when I decide,
I must return, again.

Patrick W Kavanagh
23/04/2014

THE LAST OF WINTER'S SNOW

Winter can be such a peaceful time in these sweet, gentle, temperate climes.
The long and restful nights bring snuggled comfort to our souls.
No more the breathless flight and dappled light of springtime as we dash around like fools.
No more the long hard days of summer's toil that bend us to our master's rules.

We are free to dawdle on as all the busy harvest days have gone, -
As none expect too much from, we who soon will turn to dust.
Our enduring and heroic bones will carry us to where we need to go.
Until the day we leave our cosy nests and take our final walk into eternal snow.

Still, we struggle to remain, - despite the call to leave by those who disregard all sympathy and pain.
We have much to give to those who have just barely, yet, begun to live.
Youthfully folly cries out for the words of wisdom which it is not ready to believe.
But our wisdom will be left, for those who wait behind, before we leave.

It is neither arrogance nor pride, which keeps us here, -
We who've had our ego stripped away with every passing year.
It is just a wish to leave this broken world a little kinder than it was before we came.
And to tell those who have only seen the scorching heat, that every drought is followed by the rain.

The pendulum will swing, and kindness and compassion will return when winter turns to spring.
The seeds which we have sown will grow again in beauty and in love.
Do not turn to hatred or despair in these dark times for light will surely come again.
This age of darkness soon will pass, and empathy will once again reside within the hearts of men.

THE EYE OF THE STORM

The storm has passed and everything I thought I knew has all been swept away.
The storm has passed and yet I am still standing here to face another day.
Battered, bruised and bloody but defiant to the last,
The future only opens up when we have swept away the past.

All around me lie the tattered remnants of my dreams.
An all too clear reminder that the world is never as it seems.
The sturdy trees I thought would stand forever lie with ancient roots exposed.
Too old and brittle to withstand the storm, - they could not bend to fate and were deposed.

Hearts can only break when they've already turned to stone.
Love can only hurt when we have cut it to the bone.
Lies are promises we make before we truly count the cost.
Tears are all that's left when finally, we realise what we have lost.

The storm has passed, and I am stronger than I ever was before.
The path before me seems a little clearer and my future is an open door.
I will do what I must do before my longed-for rest is due.
For still I cannot leave this world behind when there is much that I must do.

Soon the storm returns and even vanity and courage may be swept away.
The spectres of the past are screaming out to me from bitter biting winds.
Truth is finally revealed when flesh is stripped from sinew and from bones.
A skeletal reminder that no matter how we live, - we die alone.

Once more, I raise that broken tree and carry it to where a man may rise.
We can see much further when our broken hearts are lifted to the skies.
Looking down from such a godly height we see our well-planned path was simply Follies flight.
Finally, our tender hearts are ready to go into that congenial night.

Patrick W Kavanagh
16/05/2017

I AM READY TO LEAVE

I am ready to leave, for the fear has passed away and there is nothing left to prove.
I am ready to leave, for the time has long already passed, for all that binds me here.
I am ready to leave, -the knots that held me have all frayed, they lie in tattered shreds about my feet.
I am ready to leave,
The nails that pinned me to this tree, have long since rusted back to dust,
And I am free.

I am ready to leave,
My burdens cease to bother me, their weight has stripped my nerves of pain.
My burdens soon will find another beast to carry them, when I have gone away.
Responsibility lies lightly on my brow,
I care not what they do or say, - my time is over, anyway.
It is just the fear of coming back, that kept me here until today.
But still, my time to leave has come, -
No matter what you say.

My time to leave has come.
Let the bailiff knock upon my door and tell him that he missed me.
Laugh for me, and tell him, he is far too late.
Let the hounds of fate come baying at my gate, -
Their howling does not bother me at all.
Let some other take the fall, -
I have washed away the writing on the wall.
My time to leave is here,
But I shall be watching, and I will be deeply touched,
If you should shed a tear.

Patrick W Kavanagh
23/01/2013

I AM ME

I thought that I had nothing left to say.
The walls which grew between us, made me think I did not want to stay.
Exile seemed a better choice than living in a world where all my dreams could never reach the light.
I had such dreams of far-flung worlds where all was goodness and delight.

But your dreams were my dreams, - once upon a time.
The stories that I told were true, although I may have made them up for you.
In our hearts we know we meant no wrong, although we could not see the way ahead.
With only courage left, we carried on when all our dreams were dead.

We have not lost a single thing in this strange world where everything is gain.
The love which we cannot quite see, just yet, is just beyond our pain.
Even if the words I speak are false there's not a single thing that we might lose,
by living life as if it was a gift and choosing all the brighter colours which there are to choose.

I am neither fool nor saint. I have no secret wisdom which was passed from far above,
Except for that wisdom which the universe endows to everyone who looks in gratitude and love.
Each woman and each man find wisdom framed in words that they can understand.
Then they argue, and they fight as if their little piece of the puzzle was proposed for every man.

Just be happy in your own peculiar way.
In the end when all my words are spent, - there's nothing else to say.
I wish you laughter, joy and many happy years.
I can no longer waste my life in pointless anger or in useless tears.

Patrick W Kavanagh
22/04/2017

THE FINAL DUSK

I fill my glass with golden light, -
Capturing the memories of twenty thousand dusks.
To the almost empty goblet of my life,
I add this final sunset and the end of all my tasks.
I do not crave my three score years and ten, -
This is the perfect moment for my less than perfect life to end.

I have no regrets.
I have done the things my heart has always craved to do.
Now the time has come to slip away.
My fleeting form will vanish with the rising sun,
Just like the morning dew.
And, gladly though I go, - I will cherish every moment that I spent with you.

Do not bore your gods with prayers on my behalf.
Do not make my passing dreary with your laments and your tears.
Raise your glasses and your voices, -
Send me on my way with songs and with a laugh.
If I meet your gods upon my journey, -
I will surely plead on your behalf!

Life is just a passing dream.
Death is just a brief awakening in the middle of the night.
Nothing in this world is real enough to justify your anguish or your fright.
So, laugh and play each day away,
Until the moment comes when you must fight, -
Then stand your ground and strike with all your might.

We are warriors and priests.
We were never meant to live our lives like sheep.
We have no right to stand around and bleat
While one by one we all get rounded up and fleeced.
Security is just another fancy word for fear.
The time has come to shout so loud that even those within the highest towers will hear.

Patrick W Kavanagh
02/08/2017

3 AM

You woke me in the silent hours to try to fill my heart with joy.
But joy was far beyond me as I gazed out at the stars with sulky eyes.
I heard your voices in the wind that whistled down the empty street.
And in the rustle of the wind-swept leaves, I heard the patter of your tiny feet.

Happiness is such a fickle friend when sorrow waits behind each bend.
And laughter often turns to tears before our happy day has reached its fitting end.
I search my heart for reasons, but I cannot find the reason why,
I cherish my own sadness, but I will not light the everlasting candle of my joy.

What an ardent and exhilarating light it gives when it begins to glow.
That light of love and wisdom which, someday, all life will come to know.
Time and time again you come to call me to a world which knows no tears.
And time and time again I hesitate to take that final step, - perhaps because of my own fears.

I have walked these roads for long enough to realise that life is very brief.
But still, I cannot turn my back on those I love and simply leave.
Your violet eyes and flaxen hair remind me of the one I love until forever and a day,
And we will battle darkness side by side until the day my soul is swept away.

Despite my doleful mood when I awoke your magic makes me smile.
I send you all my blessing but, once more, insist that I must stay a while.
There is much to do, although my strength is not as once it was,
But you will bear me up until the time has come when I may go with you at last.

I make a cup of tea and sit here on the laptop as I wait for words to flow.
If my future is not in your loving arms, - for me there is no other place to go.
I do not know if what is true for me is true for all,
But something in me says that you will lift me up again each time that I should fall.

Patrick W Kavanagh
07/10/2017

GAZE IN THE MIRROR

Gaze in the mirror and see who you are, -
A powerful being who was born from a star.
Stardust and Spirit in a dance we call life.
Growing and blooming from all of its strife.

Looking beyond all the sadness and fear,
You will see just a spark of the wisdom hid there.
A wisdom which stretches beyond space and time.
A knowing which is both mundane and Divine.

We are the outcrop which breaches the sea.
We are the herald of all that can be.
An ape and a deity fused into one.
A misfit who's destined to shine like the sun.

It has been a long journey from stardust to man.
A trial and a battle since life first began.
But soon, we'll awaken, - our wings will unfold.
We'll discover new glories and tales never told.

So, look into those eyes and do not be surprised,
At the visions that stretch far beyond the blue skies.
We are, all of us, prophets and healers and seers.
There's a joy which is waiting beyond all the tears.

Patrick W Kavanagh
03/10/2017

TUMBLING

The silence was unruffled by the muted ticking of the clock upon the shelf.
She lay between us like a moody mist which hid the memories of every single kiss.
The years have brought a dreariness which wore away the passion that we felt.
And yet, - of all the losses which we gained, your laughter is the one I really miss.

It's been such a long, long time since last I saw you smile.
The lack of lustre in your eyes reminds me of the pain we share.
We have not left this dusty dried up world within our own front room in such a while.
The world we used to know outside may long have ceased to be for all we care.

I remember summers, once upon a time, when there was magic in a sunlit grassy field.
We walked for miles to find a quiet spot where there was no one else around
A tartan shawl laid on the ground became a battlefield where both of us would yield,
And fall into a peaceful interlude, as, cheek to cheek, we lay upon the ground.

But now we sit and stare as if we both have rushed beyond the veil to share a musty mausoleum
Sometimes I rouse myself from reverie and try to speak, - but don't know what to say.
The days are just a burden as we sit and wait for sleep and all its promises of dreams.
I wonder if you dream of when we laughed and played and tumbled in the hay.

I see you clearly now through all the years with straw entangled in your hair.
Your clothes were in a mess and through the creases of your shirt, your passion pressed.
We slipped into the barn and in a stall, we made a nest of cast-off cares.
But when the farmer came, we had to run away as maledictions filled the summer air.

Perhaps we both have lived too long? What use is life bereft of laughter and of song.
Perhaps we died a long, long time ago when we were struck by grief and everything went wrong?
Perhaps we should have fallen on our bended knees and begged forgiveness for the crime of holding on too long,
To memories of all we had which once had made the love we shared so strong?

We had a miracle and then the miracle we had was torn away.
We had a dream, but then the dream became a nightmare in a single tragic day.
Our love created life and then that life was torn away.
The god we used to love had punished us for tumbling in the hay.

Patrick W Kavanagh
16/03/2016

MY BROTHER

My brother was a terrorist who spilt your brother's blood with his own hand.
My sister was a whore who walked the bustling streets to earn enough to buy that final fix to end her pain.
My brother was an angry child who died at seventeen and poured his anger and his blood upon his land.
My sister was just fifteen when her broken heart stopped beating and she's never, ever coming home again.

My brother was an orphan who grew up in social carelessness and who never found a place to call his own.
My sister was a troubled child who never 'fitted in' and at the age of fourteen she was lured away from family and home.
My brother slipped into his final sleep beneath an archway built of cold, unyielding stone.
My sister's lover cast her off, - and now she bears a broken heart and broken mind to match her broken bones.

My brother was a railwayman until they closed the lines and took away his pride.
My sister was a teacher when a teacher could stand tall, - but now she takes in laundry on the side.
My brother winds his almost-golden watch and watches through his window as the world goes on outside.
My sister's knitting slips away from lifeless hands. My sister slips away to find a world where no one is despised.

My brother worked the land and now he earns a wage in any way he can. The landlord doesn't want him anymore.
My sister sits and grieves for sons and husband who have fought and died in some forgotten war.
My brother lives on handouts from the church and tidies gardens at the age of sixty-four.
My sister sits and wonders why the world is such a lonely place and what the killing and the dying were all for.

My brother woke up just the other day and now he wants to build a fairer world where no one needs to face a hungry day.
He says the earth was built to share and none should starve, - while others laze in unearned luxury and live a wasted life of play.
My sister runs a shelter for the beaten and abused and helps the other lost and lonely souls to find their way.
She threw away the badge marked "victim" and she stands up strong and tall to face those battles which arise each day.

Patrick W Kavanagh
05/05/2018

THE LITTLE MATCH GIRL REVISITED

Standing in the cold and gazing in,

I see a world of warmth and beauty where the firelight casts a ruddy glow.

Beyond the frosted glass, there is a world that I will never know.

It is a world where hunger never visits.

It is a world where well-fed limbs are never bitten by the frost or snow.

Am I so evil and so unbefitting to be loved by anyone?

That I have been condemned to live a life of squalor, poverty and want?

I cannot remember any crimes committed, - other than the crime of being poor,

For which the penalty is biting pains in hands and feet from icy winds, As I lie huddled underneath a bridge or sit against a locked and bolted door.

They say there was a war about a hundred years ago.

A war where people, just like me, were butchered in their millions and were buried underneath the mud and covered by the snow.

They say these brave and foolish men gave up their lives to build a better world where all men would be free.

They told me that the brave new world for which they died would be a world where want and hunger would become a faded memory.

But I cannot remember feeling anything but bitterness and want, and misery.

I tell a lie. Once I had a family, - at least I had until my dad was sent away.

They came one night and chained him up. They sent him to a country far away.

I had a mother too, - but she was broken past repair. She wouldn't eat. She could not sleep. She could not bring herself to care.

She took an overdose and left behind her world of pills and alcohol and debts and dark despair.

She left me here to walk the unforgiving streets.

Sometimes I stop outside the windows of a world that will not let me in… and simply stare…

Patrick W Kavanagh
27/02/2018

NEVER WORRY

If your life's been a struggle since the day of your birth
Just stand at the mirror and look at you now.
Every wrinkle and scar are the proof of your worth
Like a tree in the storm, - you have learned how to bow.

You are bruised, but still strong. You are bent but not broken.
You have learned from those times when it all has gone wrong,
From the dream of your life, - you have finally woken.
Now you see all the truths which were there, all along.

You stand at the sunset, - of a life that was full.
You look back at the joys and the pain.
But many were carried away at the dawn
Who did not have the gift that you gained.

Not all had the privilege to see the sunset.
They were gone like the dew before noon.
You have lost and have won but there's much to do yet.
The battle has only begun.

Every moment remaining, - in this gift we call Life,
Is a precious resource we must joyfully squander
In laughter and love, - in compassion and kindness.
We are free now to stay or to wander

Let go of regrets and just count all our gains.
This life is a gift we should treasure
This moment is all, - so let's all simply 'Be'
And accept that each breath is a pleasure

Patrick W Kavanagh
21/04/2018

THE BEGGAR

It was the coat that drew me to his side, that cold September day.
He leaned against the wall, inside a porch that barely kept the wind and rain away.
An army coat, just like my dad's, that came back from the war.
I hoped it kept him just a warm as it kept me so many years before.

I dropped some coins into his cup to ease my passage, as I walked away.
But as I glanced into his eyes, I watched him struggle with some words he had to say.
"God is bleeding into life", he said. "And life is struggling to escape the mud.
There is nothing in this world which can be made without our sweat and tears and blood!"

His aura stank of urine and insanity, and so, I walked away until he called me back.
"Your poetry is shite!", he said, "You write of flowers and butterflies like some insipid hack!"
"What can you know, old man, of what I do and who I am?"
He said, "I've walked the lonely roads since mankind first began"

"You think that speaking nice and being good will save you from your misery and pain,
But you will walk as many roads as I and birth will come again and yet again.
Your life may be a fairy tale, but fairy tales are born in blood and sweat and slime.
The grimy, gritty glories of this world will last until the very end of time."

"You bore me with your godly prayers and clean-pressed trousers on the shiny pews.
You tire me with your candles and your bells and all your failed attempts to be a better 'you'
You drive me to distraction with your chanting and your whistles and your drums.

The only truth is you, - and what you do is what your life becomes."

"**I** became this world which we both walk and we both share.
Each moment of my birth was made of misery and pain and dark despair.
You bleed my blood and cry my tears, - for you and I are one.
This is the mystery which Man has wondered at since Mankind was begun."

"**F**orget your worries and your foolish plans and simply be!
You never will be greater than you are, for I am you and you are me.
The measures and the rules with which you gauge your lives are false beyond compare."
I closed my eyes to still my spinning head, but when I looked again, he was no longer there!

Patrick W Kavanagh
25/03/2018

JUST IN CASE

Just in case I never get the chance I want to say I love you now.
We always mean the best in what we do, but words get jumbled up along the way.
Despite our best intentions, time slips quickly by, somehow.
So, I just want to use this poem to say the things I never got to say.

"Thank you!" to my sisters for your love and care when I was just a brat.
You kept me warm and fed when there was no one else to care,
I never really thanked you then for all your love because I was a twat.
But every time I fell, - I only had to call and you were there.

To those un-named people who were sent to teach me how to fight
Broken bones and broken hearts will always heal in time.
My one admission has to be that none of us were right.
So, it's been forgiven and forgotten for a long. long time.

For all those lovely people who have helped along the way,
Those priceless friends who helped me see the best of what the world can be,
You have done so much for me there are no words that I can say,
That could ever make you realise how much you meant to me.

Despite the scars, the Fates were kind, - They sent two angels who have travelled by my side.
My gratitude will never fade for such a gift which was so ill-deserved.
They steered a course beside me even when we faced the raging tides.
The love I bear for them within my heart is love that I can never, ever hide.

To all the people who have simply drifted by and neither helped nor harmed.
I wish you all a happy life, that's filled with kindness and with joy.
To all those trolls who simply seemed immune to all my wit and charm,

I take this opportunity to simply say goodbye.

NO ONE SAID IT WOULD BE EASY

No one said it would be easy when the doctor slapped your ass and sent you on your way.
No one said it would be easy when the preacher filled your mind with terror as he spoke of judgement day.
No one said it would be easy as you struggled with the bullying and jeering every day you went to school.
No one said it would be easy when your teachers called you 'idiot!' or 'fool!'

No one said it would be easy when you took a job and earned your first weeks' pay.
No one said it would be easy when you left the life you knew behind to live in your own way.
No one said it would be easy when the bills poured in and work left little time to rest or laugh and play.
No one said it would be easy, but you knew you'd somehow, someday, find a better way.

No one said it would be easy when you raised a family and first discovered sleepless nights.
No one said it would be easy when the love you knew became an endless line of silences and fights.
No one said it would be easy when your vigour and your strength began to wane.
No one said it would be easy when your body turned into a wrinkled shell beset by aches and pains.

No one said it would be easy, but you lived your life with courage and with pride.
No one said it would be easy, but you always did your best to show your better side.
No one said it would be easy, but each moment of compassion was a burning beacon which you left upon the way.
No one said it would be easy, but you've earned your rest and you are free to go or free to stay.

Stay a while, now that you're free to sit an and watch the morning sun arise while others drag themselves into the day with sleepy eyes.
Stay a while to tell your tales and see the look of wonder in the little children's eyes.
Stay a while, - The world you left behind is yours alone to cherish and to savour every happy memory.
Stay a while,
and share your wisdom,
with a world that's yet to be…

Patrick W Kavanagh
05/05/2016

ABOUT THE AUTHOR

Patrick W Kavanagh began writing after the passing of his late wife. He was encouraged to share his work on social media and found it to be a source of healing for himself and others. He now lives in Lincolnshire with his partner, Tina and their cat, Luna and Finley, the black Labrador. In their spare time they hold sound healing workshops and shamanic drumming circles.

Other works by Patrick include:

FROM THE MUSE

THE KING OF THE FAERIES

FINDING YOUR OWN WAY

KIARA

Made in the USA
Columbia, SC
27 November 2018